BASTIEN PIANO BASICS
SUPPLEMENTARY

GW00455753

BASTIEN PLAY-AL(
Familiar Favorites

Jane Smisor Bastien, Lisa Bastien, & Lori Bastien

Preface

Familiar Favorites from the *Bastien Play-Along* series is a collection of well-known songs from around the world that allows students to sample and explore a rich musical heritage. *Familiar Favorites* Book 1 contains pieces at the Primer Level and Level One. Accompaniments are provided to make learning the pieces even more fun and rewarding! We hope students, teachers, and parents enjoy this glimpse into our nostalgic past!

Sincerely,

Jane Smisor Bastien, Lisa Bastien, and Lori Bastien

You will see these icons above each new piece in this book. The circled numbers inside the icons indicate which track should be used with each piece. The metronome number at which the accompaniment has been recorded is shown under the track number. The compact disc can be found inside the back cover, and more information about the CD may be found on page 2.

ISBN 0-8497-7309-1

About the *Accompaniment Compact Disc*

The CD for this book can be found attached inside the back cover of the book. The *Bastien Play-Along Familiar Favorites Accompaniment Compact Disc* was created to musically enhance student practice sessions and improve understanding of phrasing, balance, rhythm, and pulse. Each piece in *Bastien Play-Along Familiar Favorites* includes one CD track, recorded at a moderate practice tempo. The tempos allow students to use the accompaniments **as they learn** each piece, rather than waiting until the particular challenges of a piece have been mastered.

Each piece on the *Accompaniment Compact Disc* is preceded by a two measure count-off. On the first beat of each count-off measure, a metallic triangle "ding" is heard, followed by wooden stick "clicks" on the remaining beats of the measure. Once the music begins, tempo will vary as dictated by the markings in the music, such as a *ritardando*.

On each piece, background accompaniment instruments are heard on the left channel of the recording. The student piano part as it appears in the book is demonstrated on the right channel. On many sound systems, balance between the left and right channels may be changed, either by adjusting a single "left/right balance control," or by adjusting the volume of the left and right speakers individually. These adjustments allow isolation of either the accompaniment instruments or the student piano part, or modification of the blend between the two.

When first learning a piece, it is recommended that students adjust their sound systems so that the left and right channels are equal, or so that the right channel is favored, allowing the student piano part to be heard as clearly as possible. As students become more proficient playing a piece, it is suggested that they try adjusting their systems to favor the left channel, thus making the student piano part on the right channel very soft or completely silent. This will allow students to play the piano over the accompaniment without the added sound of the demonstration piano coming from the CD.

If using an electronic keyboard, it is important that the pitch of the keyboard match the tuning note found on track 1 of the CD. This tuning note is A above middle C. The reference manual of each particular keyboard should provide information on how to make tuning adjustments.

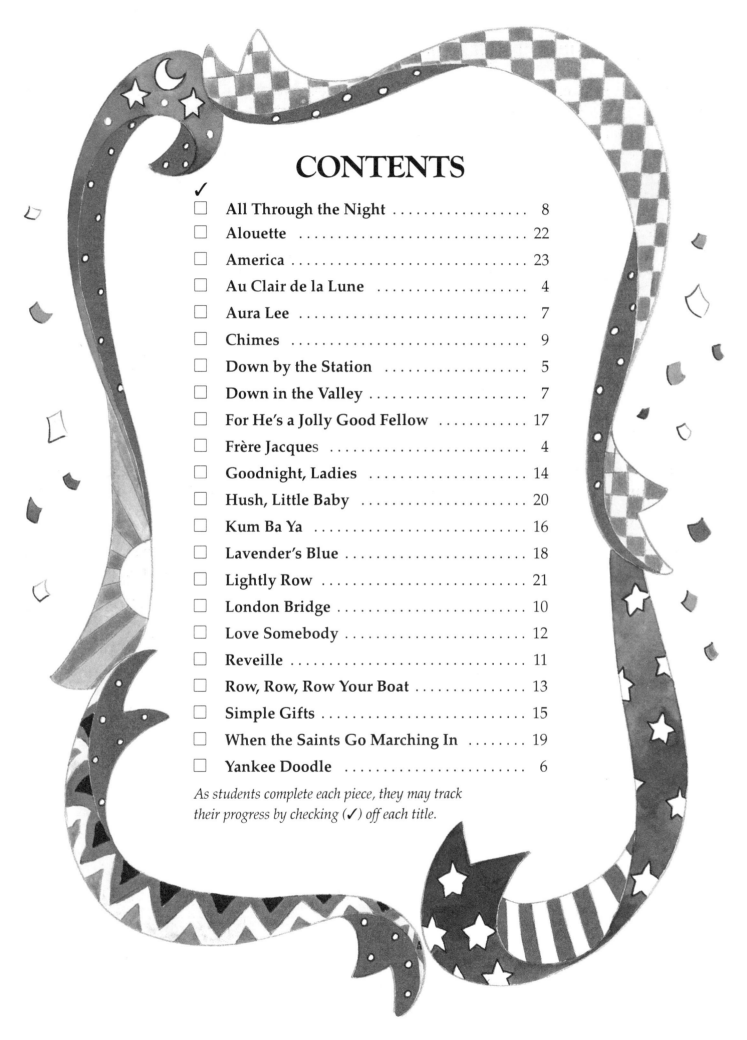

CONTENTS

*As students complete each piece, they may track
their progress by checking (✓) off each title.*

4

FRÈRE JACQUES

French Folk Song

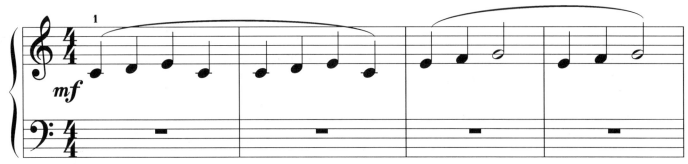

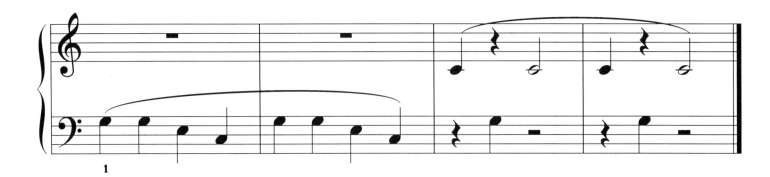

AU CLAIR DE LA LUNE

French Folk Song

KP11

DOWN BY THE STATION

Traditional

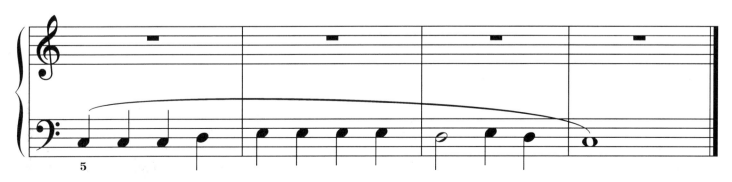

YANKEE DOODLE

Traditional 18th Century American Song

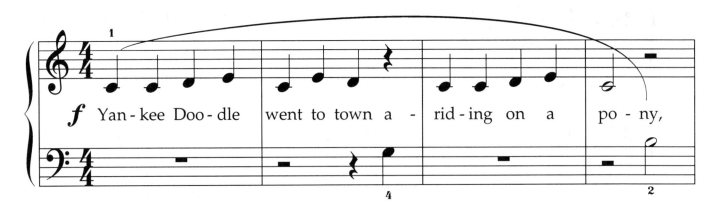

f Yan-kee Doo-dle went to town a - rid-ing on a po - ny,

Stuck a feath-er in his hat and called it mac-a - ro - ni.

AURA LEE

George R. Poulton

DOWN IN THE VALLEY

Traditional Kentucky Mountain Song

Down in the val - ley, val - ley so low, _____

Hang your head o - ver, hear the wind blow. _____

ALL THROUGH THE NIGHT

Welsh Lullaby

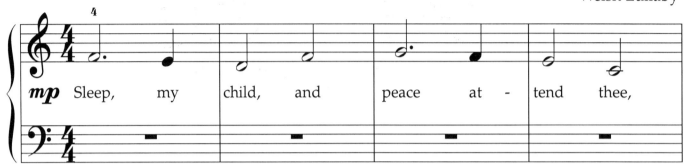

mp Sleep, my child, and peace at - tend thee,

All through the night. _____

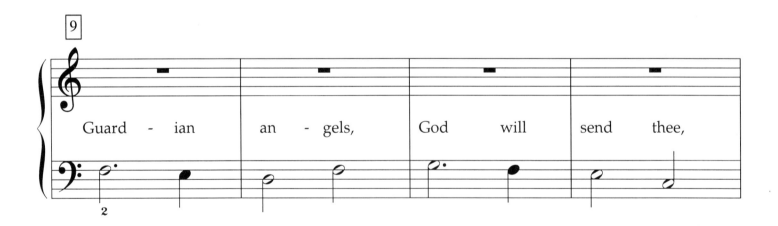

Guard - ian an - gels, God will send thee,

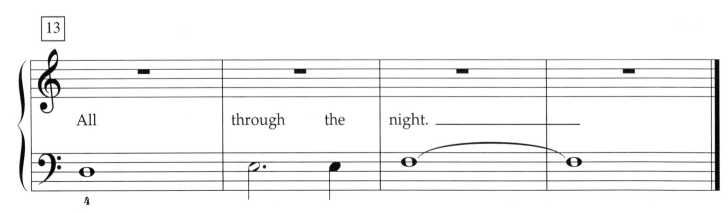

All through the night. _____

CHIMES

Westminster Quarters

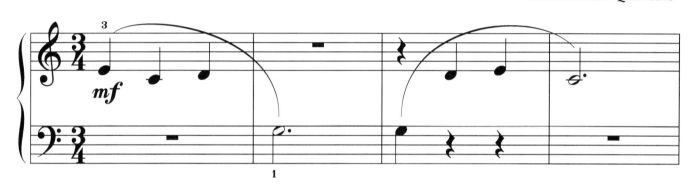

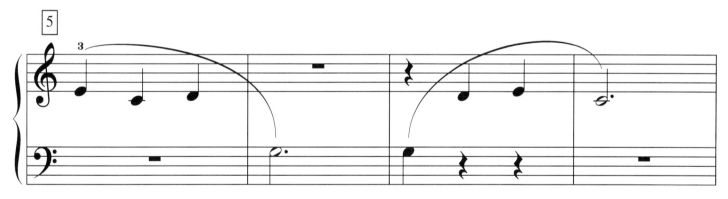

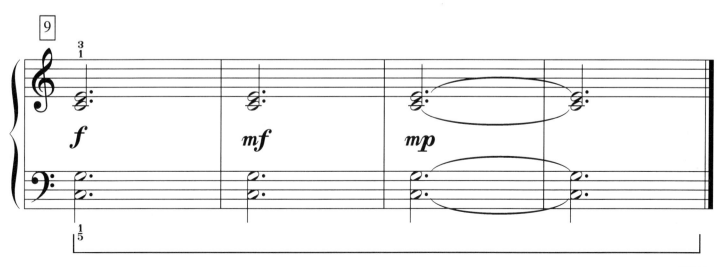

LONDON BRIDGE

Traditional English Folk Song

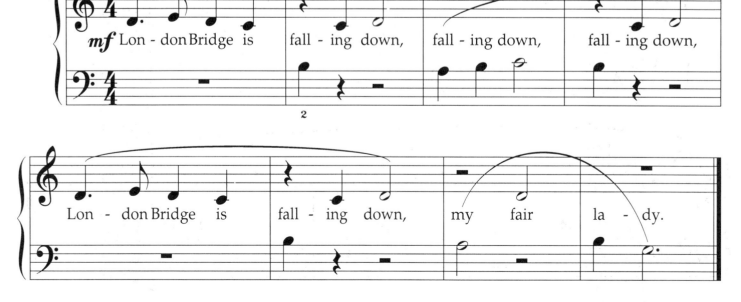

mf Lon - don Bridge is fall - ing down, fall - ing down, fall - ing down,

Lon - don Bridge is fall - ing down, my fair la - dy.

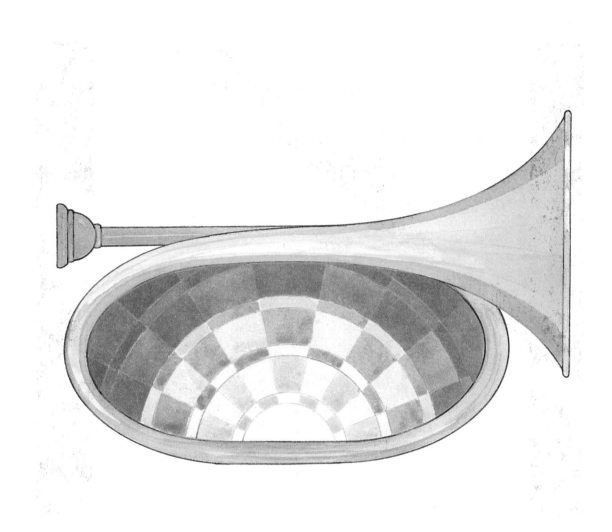

REVEILLE

♩ = 72

Traditional Bugle Call

LOVE SOMEBODY

Traditional Song

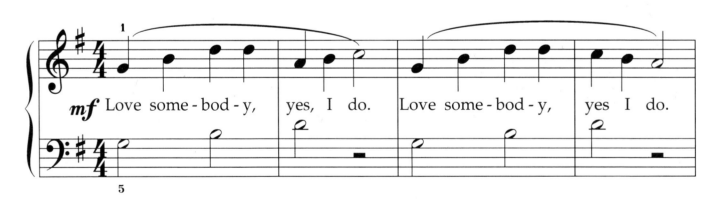

Love some-bod-y, yes, I do. Love some-bod-y, yes I do.

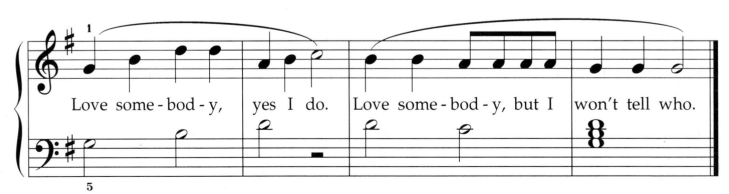

Love some-bod-y, yes I do. Love some-bod-y, but I won't tell who.

ROW, ROW, ROW YOUR BOAT

Traditional
Round

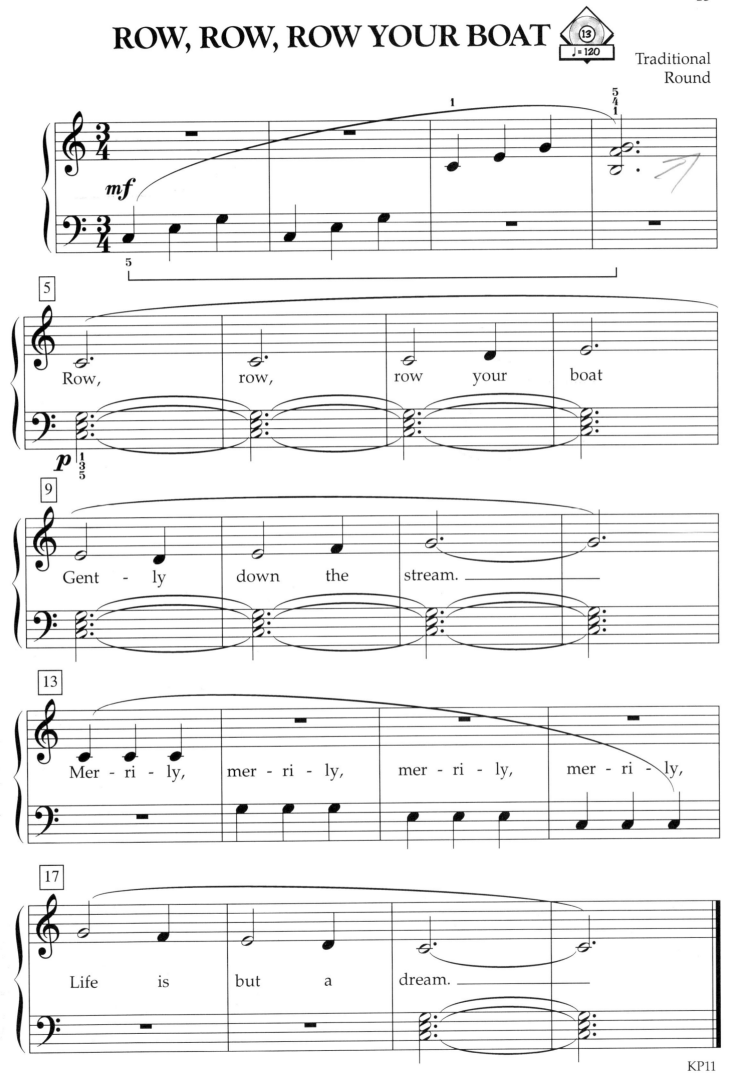

GOODNIGHT, LADIES

with *Merrily We Roll Along*

Words and Music by E.P. Christy

Good - night, la - dies, Good - night, la - dies,

Good - night, la - dies, we're going to leave you now.

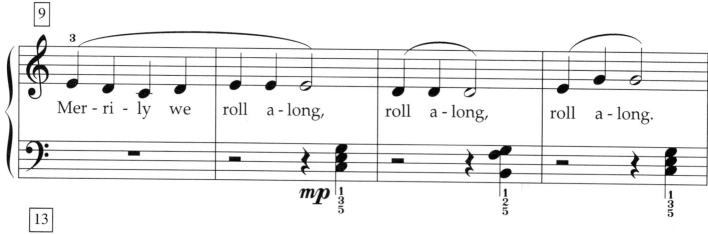

Mer - ri - ly we roll a - long, roll a - long, roll a - long.

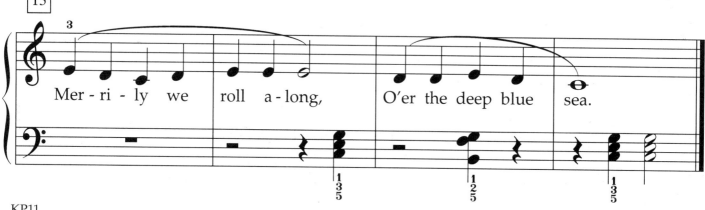

Mer - ri - ly we roll a - long, O'er the deep blue sea.

SIMPLE GIFTS

Shaker Melody

KUM BA YA

African Spiritual

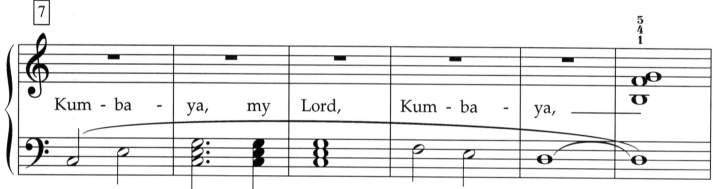

KP11

FOR HE'S A JOLLY GOOD FELLOW

Traditional English Song

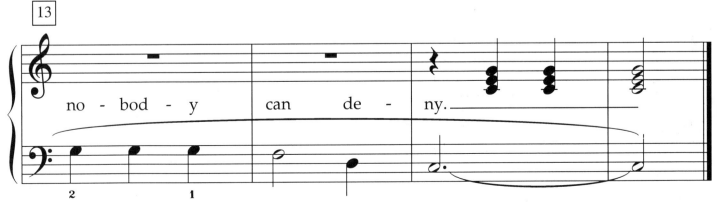

LAVENDER'S BLUE

English Folk Song

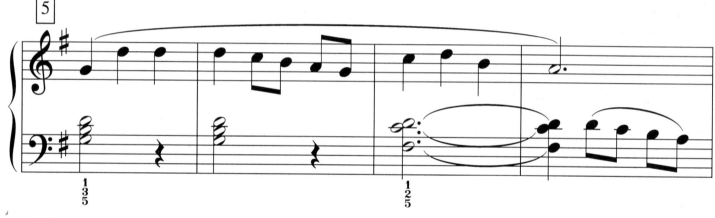

WHEN THE SAINTS
GO MARCHING IN

Traditional African-American Song

HUSH, LITTLE BABY

Traditional Lullaby

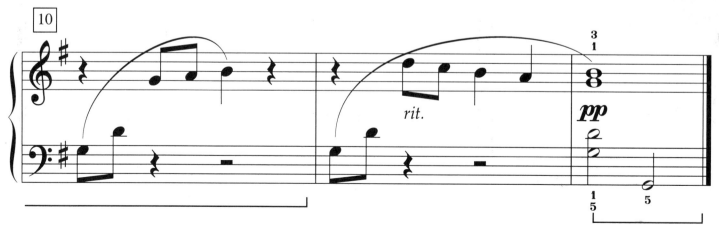

LIGHTLY ROW

Traditional Folk Song

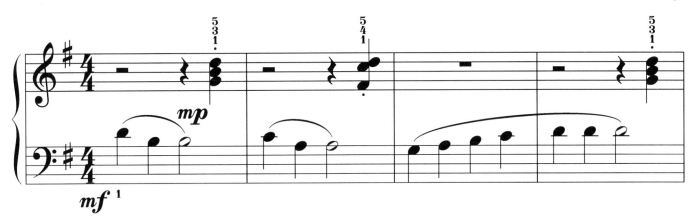

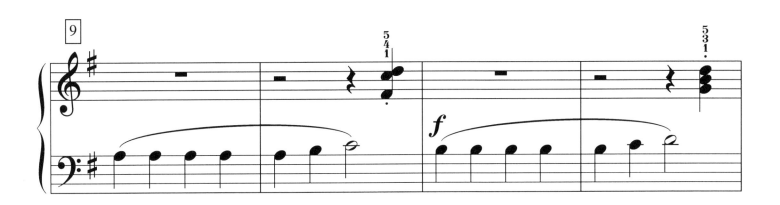

ALOUETTE

French-Canadian Folk Song

AMERICA

Words by Samuel Francis Smith
to the tune *God Save the King*

a tempo

rit.

mf

My coun-try

'tis of thee sweet land of lib - er - ty of thee I sing.

Land where my fath - ers died, Land of the pil - grims' pride,

From ev - 'ry___ moun - tain-side, let ___ free - dom ring.

rit.

KP11